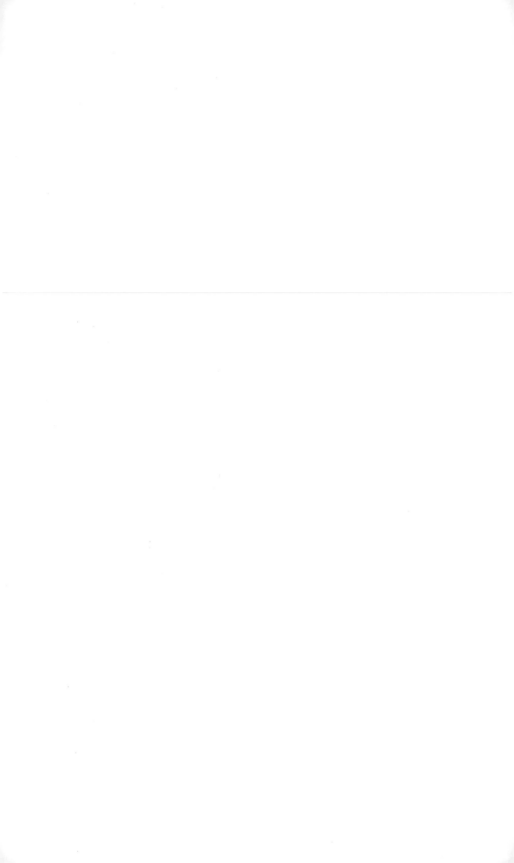

Love Is A Place
A collection of poetry

by Arlene Sundquist Empie

Boulder House Publishers
La Conner, Washington 98257

Love Is A Place: A collection of poetry

Copyright © 2011 Arlene Sundquist Empie
First published in the United States of America

All rights reserved

No part of this publication may be reproduced in any manner whatsoever without written permission except in the case of brief quotations embodied in critical articles and reviews. Address inquiries to sunnie1@me.com

Love Is A Place
/ Arlene Sundquist Empie — lst. ed.
p. cm.
Library of Congress Control Number 2011960285

ISBN 978-1-931025-09-6 Paperback

Published and printed in the United States of America

FIRST EDITION

10 9 8 7 6 5 4 3 2 1

Although the author and publisher have made every effort to ensure the accuracy and completeness of information contained in this book, we assume no responsibility for errors, inaccuracies, omissions, or any inconsistency herein.

Photographic credits: Marielle Blanc, cover design, p. 53
                      Kristen Burrows, pp. i, vii, 30, 36
                      Hart W. Empie, pp. x, 9, 15
                      Illustration Julien Blanc, p. 11

Photograph by Anna Hoover

Arlene Sundquist Empie

Author of *The Legacy of Ida Lillbroända: Finnish Emigrant to America 1893*, which was awarded National Best Books Awards 2010 Finalist multicultural nonfiction and narrative nonfiction; Winner 2011 Indie Book Award; Silver Medal Ben Franklin Award, and Bronze Independent Publishers IPPY Award. *Minding a Sacred Place,* written under author pen name Sunnie Empie, received IPPY Award 2002 for architecture.

Sunnie received her Bachelor of Arts degree from The Evergreen State College and Certificate for Narrative Nonfiction Writing from the University of Washington. Granddaughter of Nordic immigrants, Sunnie credits her love of place, inherent attitude and advocacy for Nature to her Finnish ancestry. Poetic prose and poetry provide an avenue for reflection on universal relationships and place.

From her writer's studio on an island in the San Juan archipelago, thought and memory meld into twilight moments overlooking the Salish Sea.

Why do I write?

An accumulation of life experiences gives me permission. Passion makes it possible. Poetic prose and poetry allow manifestation of emotion, like a spirit being appearing in visible form.

My poem "Paloverdes Weep" and my first published prose originated far from my Pacific Northwest homeland while living in Arizona for two decades in the verdant upper Sonoran Desert, home to many indigenous species from the tiniest bird *Phainopepla nitens,* whose survival depends on mistletoe that grows on paloverde trees, to towering saguaro cacti. But what was once pristine desert landscape was being rapidly transformed by land-hungry developers. Asphalt-covered strip malls and subdivisions with names like Terra Vita (earth and life) mocked the desert's former presence.

The scene that prompted me to write my first published story remains vivid: Beside the road lay a huge twisted pile of freshly broken tree trunk and limbs. I stopped the car. Tears filled my eyes, but I was not alone to mourn the tree's brutal death. Across the road, an old gray pickup pulled up alongside the mangled remains. A gray-haired man wearing gray overalls stepped from his truck. He stood beside the remains of the blue paloverde that had just been ripped apart by the scraper's blade and with his hands to his face, he openly sobbed. The magnificent blue paloverde tree, a century old or more, was the harbinger of spring in the high desert, the first to bloom in all its splendor among other paloverdes. People came from miles around to see the trees in bloom, a sea of gold so bright your eyes would squint.

The death of the paloverde tree was not a natural demise of Nature's perfect specimen; this was murder. A glaring example of human disconnect from a place to love and share with all living things. I was compelled to write about the wanton destruction of this unique desert environment, as cacti toppled under the bulldozer's blade. Back and forth, the powerful machine would manipulate the tall anthropomorphic saguaro, its arms flailing against the sky in a human-like attempt to fend off an attack by its brothers, arms reaching upward, pleading for help. Then, that wrenching, crunching sound of separation from Mother Earth and the distinct odor of virgin earth ravaged by the penetration and breaking of the desert's protective centuries-old microbiotic crust.

As I watched the ongoing devastation, I was gripped by intense emotion: *I can't take this anymore!* What can one person do when state and local government mentality is so fixed on land development that consideration of ecological consequences has no place in their grand plan? My answer: Write.

This Pacific Northwest native began writing with passion while in the Southwest; therefore, I begin this collection of poetry with desert expressions. Then, circling back along a familiar path to the blues and greens of sea and sky, forest and ferns, I continue to write from my studio beside the Salish Sea where thought and memory meld into twilight moments.

I bow to Nature and give thanks.
—Arlene Sundquist Empie 2011

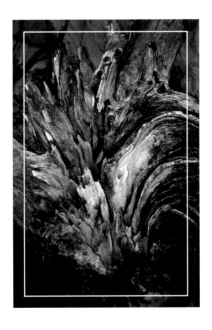

CONTENT

Part Three: Love is a Place in the Heart

A Place in the Sonoran Desert

The Scream
(with apologies to Edvard Munch)

Like the slow-moving
menacing form of a tornado
land developers' bulldozers
scrape the pristine desert
      bare of life.

The gods are angry
clouds gathering around us.

I hear a hollow, trembling sound
not the engines of heavy metal
coming down on Mother Earth.
It is Mother Earth herself, moaning
      as life is taken from her.

An odor rises from the ravaged virgin earth
like dried menstrual blood.

The wind picks up the moan
gathers the sound into a crescendo
that encircles the boulder outcrop
and from the open mouth of a stone cave
      comes a scream.

Paloverdes Weep

Quietly at dawn, the paloverdes weep,
their silken strands of tears
      reach down and touch the Earth.

      A soft morning dew clings to the wispy strands
      as Earth awakes to the Sun's first rays.

Swaying to the rhythm of the break of day
sunlight highlights their tears.
      A vertical rainbow with all the colors dancing.

      A symphony of the strands of tears
      as the paloverdes weep.

Where Have All The Trees Gone?

I breathe out, the trees breathe in
but where have all the trees gone?
The lungs of the Earth
that cleanse the air by photosynthesis.
My thoughts and lungs begin to hyperventilate
as I look out over desert scraped bare; gone are
evergreen paloverdes, deep green mesquite
and the soft lavender of ironwood blossoms.
Trees don't leave with the seasons like snowbirds
or as flowers or trends go; they continue to grow
and support us as long as they live. But in this time
of land deals and master-planned developments,
their lives are cut short, as ours may yet be.

The animals truly sang across the desert the morning after the city council responded to community effort, listened to the people, and voted to stop proposed master-planned development that would have allowed devastation of 1,000 acres of pristine upper Sonoran Desert for strip mall, golf courses and subdivision of homes to be named after an Atlantic fish.

Across a Desert Morning

Something arose
    with the first light of dawn
Something
    in the air.
The animals are speaking about it.

Listen to their voices.
Listen to the coyotes.

They came
    from the four directions.
And they sang
    across a desert morning.

Voices raised
    saluting the dawn of a new day
    saluting the dawn of a new era.

Animals talking.
People listening.

Sacred Datura

Sacred Datura, a glorious plant
as old as the Sanskrit word *dhattura*
trumpetlike blooms, perfect as my Lilly
thorny seed pods, protected by God's design
broad green leaves, bold and shiny
soaking up the sun's rays, shading a small rabbit
receiving Earth's energies and giving back.

They don't belong here, not here,
early white settlers in Jamestown said.
They're weeds. Jimsonweeds.
They don't belong here. Not here.
They tried and tried to remove this weed.
Gardeners ripped their roots from the ground
methodically, resolutely,

Earth's sacred plant resolved to stay
hugging the hillside, blooming brightly
a divine essence of an ancient time
their long ivory trumpets raise skyward
saluting the sun, heralding a new Earth spirit
moving in concert with the soft caress of wind.

The difference is human perspective.
They belong there. Here.
Where their roots have been recreating for centuries
where we can hear their ancient song.
Come, listen, to my sacred garden.

*C*oyote Survives

In spite of bounties,
poisons, development,
whatever means humans take
to eradicate this creature,
coyote survives.

Raising her head
from the waterhole,
looking us straight in the eye,
she walks away,
a parting glance over her shoulder,
coyote survives.

Good Morning, Coyote

I sit at the edge of an arroyo
in the high Sonoran Desert
watching the changing palette
of a winter solstice sunrise
sipping black Sumatra coffee
listening to the melancholy rhythm
of a desert morning. For millennia,
water carved its path around
sculptural Precambrian granitic boulders
in its westward journey, now
a meandering dry pebbly wash.
Warmed by the sun's first rays,
sheltered by jojoba, catclaw and creosotebush,
I bow to the beauty and symmetry
of a pristine desert landscape.
A soft wind rises to greet the sun.
A sweeping breeze combs
through a velvet mesquite tree.
Coyote's appearance startles me.
She stands only a few yards away,
long, coarse hairs on her shiny coat
glistening in early morning sunlight.
She slowly circles me.
I remain still, quieting my breath.
I sense this awe-inspiring creature
behind me, and I wait. I cautiously turn.
Her small face peers at me over a brittlebush
—ears poised and pointed.
I interrupt our lengthy gaze:

Good morning, Coyote.

I had awakened that morning to hear
precious water in the arid desert
flowing from the well through an open tap.
A short, jagged piece of rubber hose
dangled from the hose bib, the remainder
of a bright green garden hose
stretched out through desert bursage.

Coyote, are you the one who chewed off the hose
at the spigot, dragged it toward your den,
thinking you would have an unceasing supply of water?
What an ingenious idea.

Unconcerned with my musing,
she raises her head, catches a scent
and quickly sets her pace as she stealthily
descends into the narrow, dry desert arroyo,
makes her way down the serpentine path
to continue her search for breakfast,
perhaps an unsuspecting rabbit.

The evening the letter arrived announcing publication of my poem Diamondback in *Least Loved Beasts of the Really Wild West*, Diamond Lil, a beautiful Western Diamondback rattlesnake about three feet long, appeared in the darkness of a desert night. She had given me a poem. Did she come out of her den to claim her congratulations?

In the dark, I place a candle in each of the farolitos along the pathway. I light the first candle; the match goes out as I reach into the second can, so I strike another. Out of the corner of my eye, I sense a dark shadow beside the can, as I continue on to light the third candle.

Bill appears with a flashlight and loudly exclaims, *There's a rattlesnake out here!*

He shines the light on the second can and sure enough, there lies Diamond Lil, tightly coiled. My hand carrying a lighted match within inches of a rattlesnake would likely be threatening, but she did not move or rattle a warning.

I often greet her when she comes out to bask in the sun. Diamond Lil and I share this landscape. She is my friend and my protector. It is good to have relationships with earth's creatures.

Diamondback

Which way did you go today?

I saw your track in the sand
Wide and curvy
The soil caressed by your heavy deliberate turns
Slowly wending your way to a destination.

A considerable trek after a long winter's nap.

$\mathcal{S}$nake Lovers

He caresses her back with his tongue as his head moves slowly upward along her body. He places his head on top of hers and gently pats her head as he holds her firmly in his embrace.

An excerpt from a Harlequin romance novel? No, the courtship of two rattlesnakes. On the first day of spring, the air is alive with the buzz of a warm afternoon in the upper Sonoran Desert. A nonnative desert denizen, I share the jumbled mass of boulders that surround our home with rattlesnake, chuckwalla, Gila Monster and lizard. They command respect; I admire and enjoy their presence, although at first introduction, I was apprehensive like most newcomers to an unfamiliar wild place.

I lean over the adobe patio wall, and there lies a Western Diamondback rattlesnake about five feet long, the distinctive diamond design so vivid, and so close, that I see the sun reflected in his dark eye. We are locked in each other's gaze.

The heavy-bodied rattlesnake ignores my presence and meanders toward a smaller rattler. He nudges the base of her tail with his head. She appears disinterested in his amorous behavior as he slowly moves his long form upward over her outstretched body and strokes her back with flicks of his forked tongue. He rubs the crown of her head with the underside of his jaw, recoils and repeats the foreplay. Suddenly, her striped "coontail" curls upward like a come-hither gesture and remains bent while he deliberately maneuvers his body to wrap his tail around hers in a mating position. She slaps her black and white appendage across his broad muscular body. Excitement or impatience?

Their tails lashed together, the male continues to mildly recoil and move upwardly to caress her body and gently pat her mosaic skin, while his head and tail pulsate. She occasionally interrupts his love pats as her tail flails upward. The rhythmic body movement ceases after half an hour; he rests his head upon hers. Two rattlesnakes, their tails still wrapped together, lie perfectly still in the sun for an hour. Part of the male's body lost its brilliant color; the dark diamond-shaped markings on his lower back, muted and pale.

I sit quietly on the wall mesmerized by the sensuous scene and with mild disbelief that I was privileged to witness the union of two of earth's beautiful creatures. Slightly mystified, too, about this natural occurrence: A year ago at vernal equinox—and the year before— this same pair of Western Diamondback rattlesnakes came together beside the boulder—on the first day of spring.

$\mathcal{D}$esert Food Chain

The serene sound of the warm desert succumbs
to a major melee under a bursage bush. Camouflaged
by compatible colors of flora and fauna I know not
who or what the disturbance is about until the
shrill cry of a wounded rabbit pierces the afternoon.

> *Red Racer's wide disengaged jaws have ingested*
> *half of a small rabbit, the half not crying for help!*

Roadrunner appears and forcefully attacks Red Racer—
leaping, dive-bombing, stabbing at the snake's head
with its beak. A mouthful of rabbit impedes Red racing.

> *Am I about to witness Roadrunner swallow a snake*
> *which it can, and what about rabbit?*

A furious flurry of fur, feathers and snakeskin until
finally, each relinquishes his right to an evening meal.
Red Racer and Roadrunner retreat, leaving behind
the pathetic sight of a dazed, half-moistened rabbit
as the coolness of the desert evening descends.

$\mathcal{A}$ Mindful Connection

Gravel splays as I wheel my car around the tight turn,
pull into the open carport, stop, remove the key and look up.
Directly in front of me—a six-point buck. He stands as still as a hot
afternoon in the Upper Sonoran Desert between evergreen paloverde
trees, looking at me over a creosotebush.
I cannot take my eyes away, nor do I wish to.

I assure myself this is really happening, the deer is alive, not a
presence in my imagination. I smile weakly as I even consider this
masterpiece of art is a surprise new sculpture.
I count the points on his rack; one tip is broken.
I study the negative space between points and pair of antlers.
My eyes slide over his graceful head; my hands stroke the creamy

tan hide and feel the curves of his neck and muscular body.
Minutes pass. I impose human values on the stoic animal.
What is he thinking? Why didn't he run?
Is that a pleading look in his large, dark brown eyes?
Is he telling me the animals have had it with human behavior,
the raging destruction of the verdant high desert—an acre an hour?

The deer continues to look at me, eyes unblinking,
not a ripple of a muscle. Then the extraordinary happens.
My mind penetrates the buck's translucent dark brown eyes, or
could it have been the deer that entered my being?
A sense that goes beyond being locked in each other's gaze.
The boundary between animal and human dissolves. We are one.

After a timeless moment, the deer turns its massive body on
the gravel path, moves slowly away along a narrow animal track,
and disappears into the winding dry arroyo. I step out of my car
to follow the buck. I see nothing of its presence.
Not even the stir of branches that it passes by, or tracks.
Only the desert landscape remains unchanged.

The raven is a common iconic figure in the Norse mythology of my ancestry. The god Odin had two ravens named Huginn and Muninn, "thought" and "memory" respectively. Odin gave them the ability to speak. The two ravens sat on Odin's shoulders and delivered to his ears all that they heard and saw. Ravens are remindful of ancient myths that remain within our blood memory. I dip into the well of remembrance and find that the mytho-poetic power of the old Nordic deities can still inspire transformation in contemporary seekers.

$\mathcal{R}$avens in Flight

A magnificent pair of ravens encircles the boulders.
Their broad wings make swishing sounds
      as they fly by, always together.
      Whoosh, Whoosh, Whoosh.

Together, their wings in perfect timing.
At one with the universe and with each other
      soaring upon the natural thermals
      barking their unique sound.

Together, we stand captivated inside, observing Nature outside.
Mom and Pop Raven proudly present their big babies
      then they take to the air, short flights
      between boulders and walls.

Their glistening coal-black feathers ruffled and scruffy
a startled look in their young eyes, not the assured
      smooth composure of parents in flight.

The parents' instructions and incantations are unceasing
more than any new fledgling wants to hear.
      Squa–awk, Squa–awk, Squa–awk.

Roadrunner taps on the window, competes for attention
to show off its catch, a small inert lizard
      dangling from his beak.

Turkey vultures circle slowly, patiently, overhead,
      scavengers of dead meat, awaiting a crash.

Raven family come together under an ocotillo to rest
      large beaks open wide, sucking in air
      then another excursion into the sky.

Who is more fortunate than the raven
      to walk on Earth, to take wing and fly?

Listen

Their songs are here.
The beat goes on.

Rhythm resounds
from boulder walls
and folds back onto itself.
A blend of voices, many voices
from the depths of the Earth
sing their ancient song
with harmony, with rhythm.
The soft sound of feet
meeting parched earth,
the muffled sound of voices
behind ancient masks.

They are here.
I hear them.
The beat goes on.

*F*arewell to the Desert

Farewell, beautiful Sonoran Desert, fare thee well.
We were directed here for a reason and now,
our role has come to an end. Our legacy:
organic architecture amidst a boulder outcrop
and a story that waited 700 years to be told.
Why did it take so long to tell your story?
The ancestors replied: *Everything in its own time.*

$\mathcal{D}$ear Journal,

the house is on the market   first showing ~

3:30 a.m. check the window
serious rain   in the desert   unexpected rain
     or unexpected blessing?   The chef
     will understand   or will he?

Fiddleheads thrive in the rain.

4:30 a.m. can it rain any harder?   I groan   roll over

5:30 a.m. heavy drops   inside, not outside   does not bode well
     for showing Boulder House

trudge down two flights of stairs   gather thick towels
     spread to soak up rainwater   wet towels on floor
        not a pretty sight.

Prospective buyer   soon to arrive.
     turn on fans   heat   open doors for circulation
       take a deep breath

Stone vulvaform   embarassingly moist   will he notice?

Sunrise   smells like wet earth   and greasewood perfume

8:45 a.m.   wash running a foot deep   water across the road

OMG! shiny white sports car low slung   hugging gravelly mound

      chef at the wheel   arrives early.

Beside the Salish Sea

Nature Beckons

Remembering a place within the six directions
something within me is tugging to go North
        to the sea
        to sandy beaches
        to rocky shores

        weathered limestone hugging cliff walls

        resembling the bones of earth.

To crisp morning air carrying the perfume
        of oncoming rain
        of salt air
        of kelp lazing in a flood tide

        warm driftwood on the shore

        scattered about like old souls.

The call of Nature, our soul connection to the universe
reaches back into childhood to unravel memories
        of skipping stones on still water
        of gathering shells on the beach
        of digging caves in cool sand

        kicking crisp dry leaves in autumn

        watching clouds and seasons drift by.

*K*iket Bay under dawn's blanket of fog.
Islands rising out of the morning mist
Tide circling and ebbing toward Deception Pass
Dark figures of driftwood floating languidly with the current.

Cormorant dives and disappears.

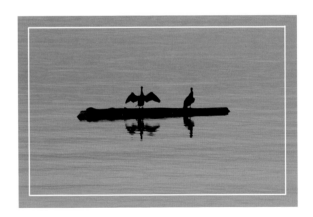

Coming Home

Coming home,
the road descends at Conway hill
through dense forests of alder,
tall Douglas fir, graceful hemlock, and
majestic Western red cedar.

The Skagit Valley comes into view
like a curtain drawn wide open
from the edge of the Cascade Mountains
to the marine-air haze
hovering over saltwater bays.

In the far distance, the San Juan Islands
like a chain of spectrolite gemstones
floating on the silver surface of the Salish Sea.
Orcas Island's Mt. Constitution
presides over the archipelago.

On the Skagit flats, checkerboard fields
like a quilt fashioned in shades of gold and green.
And there's a river running through like
a ruffled ribbon edged in dark green velvet
of evergreen trees.

Musings on Utsiladdy Bay

My thin sneakers slide over smooth rocks
blue-grey stones meeting grey water
mist rising from Utsiladdy Bay to greet the sun
blending into the morning sky.

My thoughts perceive the First People who walked this shore.
They, too, watched the gentle motion
of waves brushing sand, of water stroking stones
as tidal waters creep slowly in and out of the bay.

A small stone captures my wandering mind.
Pick me up, the stone beckons.

I cradle the round sea-polished stone in the palm of my hand
My thumb and forefinger together frame a circle—a white
ring in the smooth matte surface of a sea-grey stone.
A timeless image shaped by wind and sea.

The stone's warmth and energy flow into my hand.
Clearly, the stone has a soul and a message for me.
The subtle strength of a simple message in stone
affirms my connection to the Universe.

Put it back, I chide myself, let someone else thrill to touch
this talisman of time, but the sea-grey stone with the
perfect white circle called to me from millennia ago.
I walk away that sea-grey day, a stone tucked firmly in my hand.

Vad vill du mer? Ett vindsrum där mot söder,
en björk, en rosenhäck, ett smultronland,
en buktig flod, en fors, en bro, en strand
och kyrkans torn mot morgonskyn som glöder.
                          —*Zachris Topelius (1818-1898)*

Translation:
    What else do you need?
    An attic room with view to the south
    a birch, a rose hedge, a strawberry field,
    a winding river, a rapid, a bridge, a beach
    and the church tower glowing in the morning sun.

$\mathcal{B}$eside the Salish Sea with Topelius

Inspired by Zachris Topelius (1818-1898)

What more would you want?
A writing studio by the sea, paper and pen
a chorus of birdsongs in the morning
a sun-warmed wood bench
raspberries and cream
birch trees and rowan
aroma of cedar branches
arbutus mirrored in still water
like an impressionist painting
sea rose bowing over blueberry stones
driftwood and eelgrass
hermit crabs and tidepools
evening light filtering through fir trees
a book by my bedside
and the love of a gentle man.

In Praise of Shadows

For want of a shadow, nothing compares to
anticipation on a cloudy day, yearning for sun
like an artist's canvas awaits the first stroke of pigment,
like a writer's pen divines for words.

Sunlight breaks through clouds like a curtain opening,
reveals a brilliantly costumed cast, streaks through silver
birch highlighting paper white bark, casts its glow across
terra-cotta trunks of arbutus arching over the seashore.

The artist's brushstroke creates deep shadows on
a somber grey palette, rich colors of labradorite
dappled with brilliant white on wind tossed waves.
My mind drifts about like an abandoned skiff.

Sit down and write. Write poetry.
I grasp my pen like a divining rod seeking water,
words surface, cursive writing begins to flow
onto gleaming paper as yellow as the morning sun.

My heart pours forth love songs—to bald eagle watching
from its lofty perch atop a Douglas fir, to an octet of
Barrow's Goldeneye who return to Kiket Bay in winter,
to rosehips sparkling in sunlight and in praise of shadows.

On the Beach at Bayview

Across Padilla Bay, puffy white clouds
from tall, black smokestacks
rise and tumble one into the other
a gentle wind nudges them northward

from the oil refinery.

No reason for concern.
Steam, they told me. *Just steam*

from the oil refinery.

In the mailbox, a letter
a warning amidst mundane mail:
In case of emergency at the oil refinery
would you like immediate notice?

From the oil refinery.

I recall the night I approached the hill before home.
Western Red Cedars silhouetted against ominous
crimson clouds in the night sky. Dread rippled
through my body, like waves on an incoming tide.
A fiery cloud illumined by brilliant lights

from the oil refinery.

Riding on the waves, single loon poises so elegantly
his head erect, his pointed beak darts east to west;
north to south. What does he see? What does he hear?
Squirrel loudly chatters a warning to her kids to hide,
swallow shrilly admonishes her babies: *quiet, heads down.*

Will I hear their warnings and flee like animals before
a tsunami? Only if I am listening.

In Memoriam

In the early morning fog that hugs the
shoreline, then creeps slowly across rich
moist earth reclaimed from the sea,
her breath mingles with Earth's breath
drifts lazily through green pastures
hovers over emerald lily pads on the slough
rises upward through pale green leaves
of weeping birch trees, mingles wispily
amidst graceful branches of tall cedars and
flees into the blue-grey sky beyond, an
ethereal voice riding on the waves of the wind.

Sense of Place

As the light gently receded into night
      a small piece of weathered bark
      called softly to me.

Pick me up, it said.
      I, too, have a story to tell
      among you story tellers.

Nestled firmly in the palm of my hand
      it spoke to me.

I guarded a cedar tree
      for over 300 years
      but an unnatural fate befell me.

My limbs and trunk were scattered
      to the four directions.

But my soul is still here
      in this place
      at this time.

Thank you
      for taking the time
      to touch me.

Lillevän's Song

The master music maker stood at water's edge
heard the voice of a cedar, the Salish tree of life
entombed for centuries at river's bottom near the Skagit's
mouth where brackish water meets the Salish Sea.
He pulled and sucked the log from the river's hold
      the river relinquished its silten grasp
      the ancient cedar emerged
      silt-laden water heaving from its crusty bark.
You shall sing again my friend, he vowed. He would
recreate the tree of life in the vibrant sound of a kantele.

Väinämöinen, born of the goddess of Nature, fashioned
the first stringed instrument from the jawbone of a pike
its strings splayed outward from the teeth of the
giant sea creature like mute spaces on a harp.
The modern-day Lillevän sang his song of rebirth
      he turned the wood over and over
      with his hands he wielded his tools
      and polished with a touch so gentle
like his fingers ply the accordion to make beautiful music.
The strings resounded from his soft touch
as song receded into the tight vertical grain wood
cedar held its song and became whole again.

In the blueberry calm of evening beside the sea
I cradle and stroke the handsome kantele Lillevän gave to me.
The master carver avowed: you shall sing again,
my little friend and sing it did.
The ancient cedar buried for centuries
      in sediment at river's bottom
      regained its breath as a kantele
      and cast its mystical song.
We sing to its brothers cedar and arbutus, to its sisters
silvery birch and Sitka spruce, to the hägg and rowan,
to Great Blue Heron and grebe, while crows chortle,
Bald Eagle chitters, salmon jump into the air.

The sound of our voices reverberates across the sea
to celebrate an ancient story, circling back along a new path
like the fisherman casting his line over the water.

Cedar River Watershed: Divergent views

I

A stone promontory looms overhead: Rattlesnake Butte, looks
like elephant butte. A row of hikers stands upon its curved brow,
the elephant's long trunk descends down the ridge, back arched,
wide haunches covered with a dark green blanket of Douglas fir

silhouetted on the skyline like prickly hairs on an elephant's back.
Wide grey rippling stripes pierce the emerald green undercoat
on the pristine lake beneath the butte. Wind from multiple
directions creates a painterly image on the watery canvas.

The Snoqualmie tribe's ancient creation myth tells of this land
from the top of Mt. Si to Rattlesnake Butte.
     This land was their land,
     this land is my land.
Their legends live on— I write the legacies of white settlers.*

* *The Legacy of Ida Lillbroända: Finnish Emigrant to America 1893*

II

Watershed imagery portrays natural beauty—preserved, pristine terrain. Unsettling contrasts prevail at Cedar River Watershed: Rattlesnake Butte appears like an elephant; the new alpine lake, created by a botched dam, stocked with non-breeding hatchery trout.

On the shore, invasive plants overpower indigenous flora. Native trailing blackberries succumb as Himalaya and Evergreen vines vie for position. The guide startles me when he reminds:
This was a sacred place to the Indians.

A sacred place drained of energy and indigenous beauty. I hear drums beat, but not the drums of native people. Only Tahitian and African rhythms project outdoors through loudspeakers.

Summer in Seattle

The aroma of Starbucks, *The P–I* on the doorstep
    luxuries of a Seattle morning.

Cookouts and cook-ins, fresh herbs and vegies
    salmon from The Market.

Reading, writing, yoga and tennis, time for a walk
    exercises for mind and body.

Strollers and Pampers and kids in the park
    an exercise in patience.

A ride on the ferry, *A Slug in my Latte*,
    Hammering Man never stood so tall.

Eagles in flight and ravens soar
    in the spirit of friendship.

Surf and sand and salt-scented air.

A time to think and a place for spontaneity.

Anyone for summer?

Read on "Weekday" KUOW Radio August 3, 2001

*A*utumn

Harvest Moon hangs suspended in blue-grey twilight
announces autumn's arrival while a tinge of red
preys upon vine maple leaves like blush on a
young girl's cheeks. Unlike harbingers of spring
and regeneration, autumn assigns change.

Like an artist mixing brilliant pigments, colors
intensify to rich ruby red and medallion gold.
Magnified by sunlight, Bigleaf maples
punctuate the dark hillside, leaves clinging like
a showgirl's extravagant gold costume take

center stage against a backdrop of forest green fir.
Leaves languish as wind and time tickle their presence
drift slowly earthward, twisting, spiraling, settling
swept by winter's first breath into clusters of leafdrifts
fading to nothingness, only delicate skeletons remain.

Spiders webs, like bejeweled tapestries, glisten as
early morning sunlight caresses their mist-covered webs.
The air takes on a hollow crispness
silence and greyness engulf the valley
autumn submits to the inevitability of winter.

Picking up the Pieces

November 4, 2004

My hope for the world temporarily shattered
that November day, I call for help
but who is there to listen?

I wallow in the slough of despond
too distraught to search for a restorative poem
as salve on the wound.

I recall the sweet moments
sheltered in a circle of sensitivity
with writers, poets and artists.

Like emerald green water
heaving and whirling through Deception Pass
as the tide turns, a current of words will spill forth.

Winter Solstice Symphony

A harmonic composition of
ice crystals earthbound
melding together into
snowflakes gently
falling, drifting
disguise, soothe
anxious thoughts
like snow covers
earth blemishes
palpable calmness
permeates crisp air.
No need to guard solitude.

Winter White Jul

Outside . . .
ice on the pond
frost on the steps
snow on the path
trees draped in white
fog hovers
breath escapes
into whiteness.

Inside . . .
white clapboard house
bland and blond
food and family
jul table like
snow white landscape
white damask cloth
lutfisk, white sauce
sprinkled with allspice
white potato flour lefse
white boiled russets
pickled herring.

Ice crystals slide down
warm kitchen window.

Spring Breaks

Witness the drama of a frozen sea
stark whiteness reaches to the horizon
like a girl in a white gown arising
stretching after a long sleep
breaking the silence of winter
angular patterns of cracking ice
wild as the imagination.

Sol ute, sol inne,
sol i hjärta, sol i sinne
— Finnish-Swedish folk saying

Sun outside, sun within
Sun in heart, sun in spirit.
— Sun thought,

Love is a Place in the Heart

The poet looks at a stone,
    sees the goddess holding the moon.

Faces quietly gathering
in the twilight of memory
moving slowly and frontally
compelling faces come into focus
always approaching, drawing nearer
faces mirror a distant past into the future
they never retreat, they remain mute
for a brief moment our souls lock
and then silently and magically
they recede and disappear
into black nothingness.

into black nothingness
they recede and disappear
and then silently and magically
for a brief moment our souls lock
they never retreat, they remain mute
faces mirror a distant past into the future
always approaching, drawing nearer
compelling faces come into focus
moving slowly and frontally
in the twilight of memory
faces quietly gathering.

After the Memorial

Listening to the warm,
the warm sea aroma rising from the frothy edge of
saltwater stealing across sand, bearing new life
amid rotting marine carcasses. Nature's rhythms
like tidal waters eternal ebb and flow nurture thoughts
of love and longing. Tidal surge swells, bursts
through a narrow passage, seawater spills into the bay,
gentle waves flow steadily forth to rhythmically
climax upon the shore.

Hearing the silence,
the silence that follows a pair of trumpeter swans
raucously greeting the morning across the foggy beach
silence that lingers as two loons absorb into the beyond
anticipatory silence when eyes meet in a love embrace
poignant silence as loon calls a soulful sound across the bay
echo and loon disappear into the morning mist
silence remains, as heavy as the memorial wreath
drifting westward toward the sunset.

*E*mily and Me

Emily Dickinson and me
alone in our thoughts
alone in our rooms
writing short impressions
with poignant similarity
thinking of the lover
that was not to be hers
that I am hopeful will be mine

happy alone, not lonely
reluctant to spread our wings
beyond comfort of the cocoon
perhaps when winter pales
the lemon butterfly will flit about
in genuine rhapsody
seeking transformation
that Spring foretells
seeking a lover that longevity
health and desire require.

*R*ainy Weekend at North Cascades Institute

If not for the rain . . .
    Would we see water shimmering down
        glistening walls of stone
            water tumbling from the mountaintops
            through crevasse and swale
            like white satin ribbons
            adorning a spring green dress?

If not for the rain . . .
    Would we see magnificent waterfalls
        cascading over basalt boulders
            spilling onto the roadway
            emerald green moss pregnant with moisture
            rainwater dripping from lichens
            hanging from naked branches
            like goats beards?

If not for the rain . . .
    Could we hear the music and rhythm of raindrops
        dancing upon a metal roof?
            Steady, intense vertical rainfall
            defining architectural open spaces
            rain sheeting over lustrous grey metal
            falling freely from the roof
            into staggered metal troughs.
            A steel scupper protrudes from roof's end
            ejaculates rainwater onto glistening stones
            within a circular concrete chalice.

If not for the rain . . .
Would we know the sweetness of a moss-covered bed
beneath weeping fern fronds? Overhead,
raindrops cling to bare vine maple branches
like Swarovski crystals from a boudoir chandelier.

Spring's Song

Spring's song opens the mind to possibilities
swallows return to rebuild their nest in a flurry of activity
tractors ply the fields turning over fallow soil
preparing for new life to come forth.

Released from the long winter rainshadow, my mind jazz
dances to places charted on my journey, places yet to know,
signposts to follow. The fork in the path beckons like the rock
on the beach with the perfect circle calls to be picked up.

Places summon in my dreams, places co-created in the divine plan
await chance and synchronicity. Love, the highest energy of all,
surrounds me like swirling water in a whirlpool,
spilling over me like a waterfall, yet I cannot quench my thirst.

Sun thoughts wander amidst stones and pine needles,
silken sea grass and thorny blackberry vines, sensing
the pull of the moon, the incoming and outgoing tides
ever seeking —one more undiscovered place of the heart.

Through the Garden Window

Sunrise casts its orchid glow upon the rippled edges
of deep blue-grey clouds hovering in the West.

The sea shimmers in no particular direction – just trembles.
Lone seagull silhouetted against the pale blue dawn.

I give thanks for another day of loving
and then I see

the cymbidium blossom in the garden window.
The orchid color repeats like a passage of music in a symphony.

New leaves thrust upward in youthful exhilaration.
Long, slim mature leaves gracefully bow in thankful repose.

$\mathcal{A}$ Moment or Two in Time

I

Ancient sun symbol on a granite boulder
ferns dancing in mottled sunlight
a lush green forest embraces, enfolds
like the down of angel wings
around an intimate assignation
amidst a deep moist bed of moss.

When will I see you again?

My lover slips silently from my reverie
thick emerald moss carpets the land
envelops boulders like Mother Earth's
mound holds the gentle female rain
awaiting a 21st century moment
when dreams of a previous life will unfold.

II

We meet again upon life's stage
our eyes lock, rich in romantic remembrance
a palpable pause of delicious vagueness
the long gaze into sweetness
the past ignites a flame of emotion
illumines my lone presence

How long does time stand still before you look away?

The glow from within radiates
like a searchlight finding its mark
silence hovers large, as the audience
observes our ocular embrace
uninvited guests to an irrepressible
public display of emotional affection.

With Admiration and Affection

The architect wore black.
Elegant stature, imposing posture, mingling among his
entourage with aplomb, gesturing with graceful ease.
I sketch in my notebook as if I would not forever recall
his long cloud-white hair, thick dark eyebrows, warm smile.
The distinctive lavender aura I would not forget.
Nor the twinkling eyes that for a moment met mine.

He turned abruptly, my musing interrupted,
walked toward me. *May I sit here beside you?*
We clasp hands, perhaps we shook hands, when hands touch,
each no longer belongs only to its source, a new
boundary is cast, an invisible umbilical chord unites.
The wordsmith falters: *I traveled seventy miles to hear your words.*
I am honored, his charmingly gentle response.

That day he sat beside me,
I praised the higher power that opens pathways to possibilities.
As the poet Emerson bowed to the charm of the Rhodora:
The Selfsame power that brought me here brought you.
An emissary from my ancestral homeland, carrier of concepts
of design and sensuous buildings. A continent and ocean
separate us, yet through time and space the poetic beauty of
his words quenches my thirst.

Side by side that day we sat together,
a magical memorable moment of convergence.
I listened intently to the introduction, not hearing a word
the small notebook and pen lay frozen in my hands.
I discreetly glanced at his profile, a model set apart from
the multitude around us. I breathed his energy, his presence,
absorbed his whole being with only mild self reproach of my
brazen intrusion. My reverie gave way to a rush of moving air
as the architect rose to speak and the brush of his trousers
caressed my legs.

Like a teenage girl in love, squandering much of her time
thinking of her beloved, sun thoughts emanating from my soul
mingle with yearnings that return home with me through
a gentle female rain, remaining like an uninvited guest
who doesn't intend to leave.

At the Edge of the Salish Sea

Our dream for the future tumbles into the present
on an island in the Salish Sea where colorful kayaks
glide past seals and playful porpoises. Great Blue
Heron stands motionless at water's edge, cormorants
poise on driftwood slowly circling the bay, seagull lifts
above the beach, pauses midair as if suspended
by an invisible cord, releases clam to the rocks below
swoops down to pull a sweet morsel from the cracked shell.

In fields beyond: snow geese take to the air
their loud dissonant chorus trumps all other sound.
With morphic resonance hundreds of snow geese
soar as one being, a blanket of white lifting upward, turning,
settling, like a white robe covering rich, brown earth.
In the quiet that follows the surge of airborne wings,
my heavy rubber galoshes give voice to earth's tall thick grass
~ *Squish, Squish, Squish.*

I tread onward through an unmowed field at the edge
of the Salish Sea. Poet Robert Sund called this place:
Land of the Ish~ Swinomish, Samish, Snohomish, Stilliguamish.
Through the poet's window, The River takes refuge
in the slough before joining the sea. Tall reeds and
sea grass along the shore bow to a warm gentle breeze.
I pause and bow to the magnificence of Nature.

North of Hope

A pair of loons lifts from the calm sea
together as one, they rise into the grey sky
side by side their fluid bodies meld
into distant Hope Island

We stand motionless on the landing
in the morning mist north of Hope.
Spring teases and tempts the senses
lures my thoughts to places unknown.

Unrequited Love

Gentle rain comes and goes.
Tidal waves rhythmically lick the sand as they move
toward fulfillment and retreat. The river flows on
between watercolor boulders.

I am resigned to happiness alone, not loneliness
guarding my solitude, gazing into deep pools
a soft greeting, a warm smile played back a dozen times
a faint image reflected in my sauna mirror.

You are bound by vows. I cannot go there. I am bound
by respect, fear of losing friendship by breaking barriers.
The wordsmith—the one who delights in manipulating words
on paper, on the screen, cannot say what I long to express.

Be careful what you wish for breathes the voice on my
shoulder. *Is that within my power?* Ancient Norse folklore tells
that we cannot know what is possible for those in love. Spirits
watch over us on life's stage appearing like an aside uttered in a
whisper.

Only they know the path lovers will choose.

*A*dopt the pace of Nature; her secret is patience.
—Ralph Waldo Emerson

For Louise

On Lone Tree Bay north of Hope,
islands rise above the pewter sea in waning light.
Lone loon's haunting call echoes across the blue hour,
lingering tinges of Nootka rose and blue camas
dance on the crests of gentle waves.

Her paintbrush moves in languid strokes
across the watery canvas like a lover's caress
rust, mulberry, lavender, purple iris, colors recede
as blackness embraces the cold steel sea.

Black embodies all colors. Its energy speaks
of love, the highest energy of all.
Louise Nevelson fell in love with black:
Black is the most aristocratic color,
you can be quiet and it contains the whole thing.

On Lone Tree Bay north of Hope,
Great Blue Heron in tuxedo black rises from the beach
raucously flies alone toward the heronry.
Darkness descends.

Reflection on Connection

Across a crowded room, eyes meet, lock
in a lingering gaze that reaches into the soul.

Leaning against stone, arms touch, intense heat
radiates through our pullovers, a spiraling intention.

Is a love connection made physically or when eyes meet?
In the scent of a man? Scent of a woman? Metaphysically?

Yes, through the universe, souls make the initial connection.
So how does one avoid connecting with someone?
Don't look now, you can't.

Midnight Rendezvous

I lay upon a soft white cloud bed
nestled in the warm curves
of your puffy down body
yielding to soft caresses
feeling your satin lips
brush against mine
time stands as still
as the summer
solstice sun
when I awake
and beckon
the dream
to return.

I look in
the mirror
in the morning
to see a smiling face
framed by disheveled hair.
The face I know does not reflect
the emotions of the night. Together
the person in the mirror and I face daylight
and the difference between desire and possibility.

Thinking of You This Morning

I walk alone on a rutted country road
embraced by the valley's luminous light
caressed by morning mist and the scent of salt air
cuddled in a farmer's quilt of autumn colors.

I wish I could send you this postcard morning.

A panoramic view over the flats
blood red barns, white clapboard farmhouses
time-worn driftwood-grey granaries gleam,
illumined by early morning sunlight
treetops pierce through patches of fog
eagle's nest exposed amidst bare branches
a few golden leaves cling like autumn's last sigh.
The rising sun at my back,

I follow my lengthy shadow to where?

A gnarled wood fence, an abandoned garden
where November's red rose remains tightly clenched
holding hope that sun will bestow one more blossom
the warm sun teases and tempts the burgundy rose
to unfurl her carnal passion and bloom once more
'ere winter's first snowflakes fall upon deep red petals.

I look up through tears of joy and hope.

Formations of migrating Arctic snow geese like
runic writings in the sky, messages through time and space
black-tipped white wings glisten in morning sunlight
one flock follows another: gliding, descending, settling
like a downy white blanket on green fields
a cacophony of voices speak a language foreign yet familiar
a lyrical reminder of universal connections.

I walk alone in beauty on the open road.

Sun thought,
Walk gently on your journey.

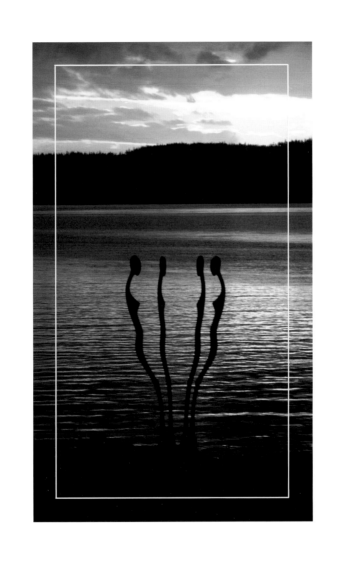

Endnotes

The title for this first collection of my poetry was in place when I came across a poem of E. E. Cummings. I bow to his sensitivity to place.
> Love is a place. Through this place of love move
> (with brightness of peace) all places.
> ~ E.E. Cummings

Poems appeared in the following publications:
"Winter White Jul," *The Quarterly*, Swedish Finn Historical Society. 2011.
"Lillevän's Song," The Finnish American Reporter. July 2011.
"Beside the Salish Sea with Topelius," *The Quarterly*, Swedish Finn Historical Society. 2011.
"Coming home," *The Legacy of Ida Lillbroända: Finnish Emigrant to America 1893*. Boulder House Publishers. 2010; The Newsletter of Skagitonians to Preserve Farmland. Spring 2005.
"Sound of FinnfestUSA2009 Cruise To Alaska," The Finnish American Reporter. 2009.
"Diamondback," *Least Loved Beasts of the Really Wild West*, Native West Press. 1997.
"In the early morning fog," *The Legacy of Ida Lillbroända: Finnish Emigrant to America 1893*. Boulder House Publishers. 2010.
"Kiket Bay under Dawn's Early Light." "At the Edge of the Salish Sea." "Sun Thoughts on the Beach at Bayview." *Padilla Bay Poets Anthology: Impressions of the Salish Sea* 1993-2006. Padilla Bay Foundation.
"Musings on an Island Morning." *Stories of the Skagit Anthology II*. Skagit Valley Writers League. 2004.
"Summer in Seattle." Read on "Weekday" KUOW Radio, 3 August 2001.
"Sacred Datura," "Coyote Survives," *Minding a Sacred Place*. Boulder House Publishers. 2001.
"Sense of Place," "The Earth is Alive," *Scent of Cedars: promising writers of the pacific northwest*, Anne Schroeder, Ed., Russell Dean & Company. 2002.

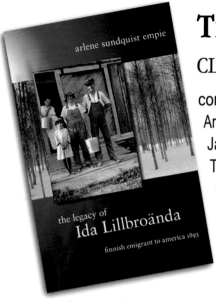

THE WEST DIDN'T CLOSE IN 1893

contrary to that which American historian Frederick Jackson Turner proclaimed. There were opportunities for adventurous Nordic women who became part of America's westward expansion.

By **Arlene Sundquist Empie,** author of award-winning *Minding a Sacred Place*

the legacy of
Ida Lillbroända
finnish emigrant to america 1893

ISBN 978-1-931025-05-8 Hardcover nonfiction $24 US
288 pages, 50 vintage photos, bibliography and index
Available at independent booksellers
Partners West, Ingram, Baker & Taylor

Boulder House Publishers
P.O. Box 784, La Conner, WA 98257
www.boulderhousepublishers.com   sunnie1@me.com

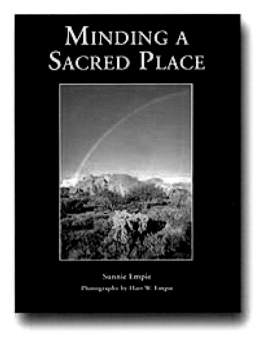

Award-winning *Minding a Sacred Place* by Sunnie Empie
Internationally acclaimed Boulder House built within magnificent Precambrian boulder outcrop. Provocative petroglyphs reveal cosmology of American Southwest's first inhabitants, ancient iconography that venerates Nature and the feminine divine. Empie Petroglyph Site AZ U: 1: 165 (ASM) National Register of Historic Places 1998.

A Sense of Place
Desert Mystique—A Spirit of Place
Creating Natural Architecture
Nature's Materials, Space, and Spirit
Boulder Approach to Architecture
Entering A Sacred Space
The Sacred Made Visible
Rock Imagery and Revelations
Caves as Sacred Places

Minding a Sacred Place, Independent Publisher IPPY architecture award 2002. ISBN 1-931025-03-7 Clothbound, 200+ pages, 150 photos by Hart W. Empie, index, bibliography. $60

Boulder House Publishers
La Conner, WA 98257
www.boulderhousepublishers.com